"Anthony Tako is a genuine follower of Jesus Christ. I was blessed to serve under his leadership as an elder in our local church. I could not think of a man more gifted by the Lord to lead as an Elder Chairman. He truly is a shepherd of the elders and the entire church body. Everything discussed in this book has been lived out in front of me."

—DAVID CORNING
Chairman, Entrusted Ministries

"This book will make an impact on the leadership of the church! Elders are called to shepherd the flock and yet, often, lack practical guidance. This exceedingly helpful book provides the necessary list to pursue God's heart as a church leader. The book fills a void by combining sound theology with practical application; a book I wish I would have had prior to my board service. Thank you, Anthony, for calling us to serve wholeheartedly and serve with excellence."

—DUANE MARTIN
Former Chairman of the Board, Greater Europe Mission

"An excellent resource for the function and ministry of Elders! Anyone who aspires to the work and ministry of being an elder will find this book a sound, clear, and excellent guide. I am very thankful for the experience and wisdom in the book."

—DAVID E. SMITH
Executive Director, Illinois Family Institute

"Books on leadership abound. Books on church leadership, not so much. There are precious few that highlight the qualifications and roles of elders, particularly the role of the elder chairman. Anthony Tako has written a helpful, practical guide to fill the gap. He is qualified to do so. With six years of experience as a deacon, and then nine years as an elder (the last three as chairman), he has gleaned a great deal of both biblical and practical wisdom. And he lives it out. I know this, because he was the chairman at my church. So, I recommend this book for anyone who has the privilege of serving as an elder, whether they have been in the role for years or were just recently appointed. It would be good for an elder board to study together, as a way of collectively honing their craft. My friend is willing to share wisdom with you. Let his pain be your gain."

—DAVID W. JONES
Senior Pastor, Village Church of Barrington

Shepherds of the Flock

Shepherds of the Flock

Key Things Elders Can Do Now
to Lead More Effectively

ANTHONY S. TAKO

Foreword by Jonathan T. Pennington

WIPF & STOCK · Eugene, Oregon

SHEPHERDS OF THE FLOCK
Key Things Elders Can Do Now to Lead More Effectively

Wipf & Stock
An Imprint of Wipf and Stock Publishers
199 W. 8th Ave., Suite 3
Eugene, OR 97401

www.wipfandstock.com

PAPERBACK ISBN: 979-8-3852-5214-5
HARDCOVER ISBN: 979-8-3852-5215-2
EBOOK ISBN: 979-8-3852-5216-9

VERSION NUMBER 07/28/25

First and foremost, this book is dedicated to my wife, Lindsay. This book is as much about your service and love for our family as it is about anything else. I wouldn't have been able to serve in any of the ways discussed in this book without your support in the background. Thank you and I love you.

This book is also dedicated to my children: Marie, Evangeline, Anthony and John. I love you all more than you could ever understand or imagine. Thanks for loving your imperfect father in the years I served in church leadership which allowed me to gain experience and wisdom to invest in this book.

Contents

Contents

Foreword

As I look back on nearly thirty years of ministry both in the church and the academy, the thread that ties together all of my experiences is *friendship*. From my first pastoral job in rural northern Illinois through the wonderful opportunities I've been given to teach in churches, parachurch organizations, theological institutes, and universities all over the world, everything good has come about through friendships, both old and new.

One such friend that spans most of this time frame is Anthony Tako. For as long as I've known Anthony, he has been the same good man—intelligent, reliable, hard-working, generous, conscientious, and faithful. All of those character traits have guided the college student I first met into becoming an incredibly successful businessman, a loving husband and father, and a faithful church leader. Anthony's character and experiences in business, family, church, and the workplace are evident on every page of this wise little book.

While the content is all his, it is my fault you're reading this volume. On a walk near his house two years ago, when talking about my little book, *Small Preaching*, we hit upon the idea of him doing something similar for lay elders in the church. Anthony has labored diligently—and graciously accepted many rounds of my feedback—to put down on paper his experience-borne wisdom. These twenty-five digestible and practical essays are designed to be of help to others as they navigate the wild and woolly world of church leadership.

Anyone who aspires to be a church leader or finds themselves in the midst of this calling will benefit from the thought and care Anthony has put into these words. I pray that this practical and Godward wisdom will reach a wide audience.

Dr. Jonathan T. Pennington

Acknowledgments

To my senior pastor, Dr. David W. Jones. You have shown yourself to be a faithful expositor of God's word, which has helped me grow in my walk with the Lord. Throughout your ministry, you have also proven to be a godly man of character. It has been a pleasure and joy to serve with you as elder chairman.

To my dear friend, Dr. Jonathan Pennington. I am grateful for you. Since I was a young Christ follower you have modeled grace for me and demonstrated how a godly man serves in ministry. Thank you for your help with this project!

To my assistant, Jo Blanchette. I am so grateful for you and your faithful support of the many responsibilities the Lord has entrusted to Lindsay and me. Also, thank you for being a faithful prayer warrior for our family and for this project.

To our dear friend, Dana Leahy. Thank you for going through the painstaking effort of reviewing this manuscript and providing fantastic feedback to make it better.

Introduction

THIS BOOK IS PRIMARILY for elders[1] and those who have been called to fill the role of elder chairman. This resource would be good for those already serving as elders, but especially for those new to the role. This book is also for church leaders who have a passion to grow in their skill set of faithfully serving the Lord through their local congregation. As I was preparing to serve as an elder, there were scant resources available on these topics. My hope is churches and church leaders can use this book to prepare well for their years of service.

My story begins with a journey over two-plus decades of spiritual growth and secular career development. After coming to faith in Christ in college, I began an accounting and finance career with an area of expertise in the technology industry. As I was growing in my faith, I was also progressing in my career. I had a desire to grow both spiritually and vocationally and, yet, I had to seek out mentorship in both; it didn't just come organically. I continually thank God for the way men invested in me. The investment of others helped me grow in grace and understanding of God's word in my spiritual life. It also helped me to grow in wisdom in my career. As a result, I was blessed to lead finance and accounting organizations for two different "unicorn" companies that were sold to large multinational Fortune 50 companies.

---

1. For theological contextualization as you read this book, my position on the role of women in leadership of the church is complementarian, and I see the Bible supporting the role as being reserved for qualified men.

On my sanctification and lay ministry journey over the last twenty-five-plus years, God softened my heart through those prior experiences to provide awareness of struggles that pastors and lay leaders have. They often feel isolated and have a need for shepherding. The shepherds need shepherds. Additionally, I was blessed to help launch an organization called the 222 Foundation (www.222foundation.org), a 501(c)3 charity that provides seminary scholarships to those seeking vocational Christian ministry, the future leaders of the church. The ministry also provides a mentor to each student partner to intentionally invest in them over their years of seminary. Currently, 222 Foundation has over fifty student partners across four seminaries. Additionally, 222 alumni are serving as pastors and missionaries in five continents.

I served in lay leadership in our church, which is a larger, multi-staff church in a Chicago suburb. In our local congregation, I served for nearly six years of lay ministry as a deacon, and then was asked to serve as an elder. When I became an elder, I wanted to "work heartily, as for the Lord and not for men" (Col 3:23). In order to do that, I wanted to seek out any resource I could find on the topic of being an elder. I found many resources available related to "biblical leadership" but did not find many resources related to biblical eldership. There are a few solid resources on biblical eldership I recommend and will include in the endnotes.[2]

After several years serving as an elder at our church, I was approached about serving as chairman for the final three years of my term. At first, my quick response was "It's a definite no!" However, the Lord worked on my heart, and I took time away and made a prayer sheet of some things I was seeking the Lord to do in my life to give me clarity on the decision. In only the way God could do, he cleared nearly every one of those hurdles and boldly answered my prayers; thus I began my journey as an elder chairman. The

---

2. A few of those resources on biblical eldership I recommend are *Biblical Eldership: An Urgent Call to Restore Biblical Church Leadership* by Alexander Strauch, *Elders and Leaders: God's Plan for Leading the Church* by Gene Getz, and *Church Elders: How to Shepherd God's People Like Jesus* by Jeramie Rinne.

Lord allowed me to serve in this capacity through some tenuous times, including the COVID years.

My hope and prayer for this book is to equip fellow elders and elder chairmen with wisdom God has graciously given me through the word, experience, and other godly people. I have divided this book into three sections depending on where an individual is at in their service as elder. The first section, "A Shepherd's Character," is the baseline biblical context for qualifications to serve as elder and tips for serving. This section is a good reminder for an experienced elder and a good starting point for a new elder, perhaps serving for the first time. The second section, "A Shepherd's Work: Shepherding the Flock," is a challenge to focus on the 1 Pet 5:2 mandate to shepherd those in our congregations and provides some tips on how to effectively do that. The final section, "Shepherding the Shepherds," focuses on elders encouraging and shepherding fellow elders, whether in the role of chairman or as a co-laborer for the Lord.

Part I—A Shepherd's Character

1. *Walk Faithfully*

As MEN, WE TYPICALLY strive for achievement and we love to know the best way to achieve a goal. In our personal lives, we can gain wisdom from other individuals that have experience on how to achieve godly success. In marriage, suggestions on how we can achieve goals often comes from our wives. Thankfully, when considering serving as an elder, the Lord provides clear guidelines of how to serve effectively directly in his word! The key focus area to effectively serve as an elder can be found in one word—character. "Character" is defined as the "aggregate features and traits that form the individual nature of some person or thing"[1] as well as "moral or ethical quality." The three main texts that define the qualifications and responsibilities of an elder are 1 Tim 3, Titus 1, and 1 Pet 5. They list no functional or skill qualifications other than "able to teach" (1 Tim 3:2). However, there are many descriptions of character traits of the individual, as well as his moral or ethical quality. That list includes:

In 1 Tim 3 *and* Titus 1	In 1 Tim 3	In Titus 1	In 1 Pet 5
• Above reproach	• Respectable	• A lover of good, upright and holy	• Examples to the flock
• Husband of one wife	• Not a recent convert		• Humility toward one another

1. Dictionary.com, "Character."

3

In 1 Tim 3 *and* Titus 1	In 1 Tim 3	In Titus 1	In 1 Pet 5
• Sober-minded	• Well thought of by outsiders		
• Self-controlled			
• Hospitable			
• Able to teach*			
• Not a drunkard			
• Not violent			
• Not quarrelsome or arrogant			
• Not a lover of money			
• Manage household well			
• Keeping his children submissive			

* Denotes skill or functional qualification

What an overwhelming list! As we attempt to walk faithfully as elders, being "examples to the flock" is an overarching umbrella that encapsulates several of the other character items.

What are ways to walk faithfully as examples to the flock?

Be a Student of the Word and a Man of Prayer

Consistent study with the word of God, preferably on a daily basis (Josh 1:8; Ps 1:2), is critical to walking faithfully. Put yourself, your family, and the congregation before the Lord in prayer on a daily basis.

4

Be Above Reproach

Lean into being highly above reproach in all things, but especially in the area of sexual immorality. Be above reproach in speech and conduct. Let people be blown away with the integrity of how you speak about others and how you treat others, including serving them. We are serving a Holy God. Let's bring him honor and praise with our speech and conduct. I will discuss more on this topic in chapter 2, "Be Above Reproach."

Be a Servant of Others

Jesus himself said that "even the Son of Man came not to be served but to serve, and to give his life as a ransom for many" (Mark 10:45). Continually serving others in the church and on the elder board is evidence of walking faithfully and wanting to "deny yourself and take up your cross and follow" (Mark 8:34) Jesus Christ. There is no role or responsibility too small for an elder to roll up his sleeves and serve in a local congregation.

Sadly, I would venture that many, if not most, of us have experienced leaders who have brought disrepute on the name of Jesus Christ through choices those leaders have made. Typically, that is because they were not personally walking faithfully with the Lord. Sadly, these character failures bring significant pain and suffering to the individual and their family that they have to confess and repent to the Lord. Additionally, these failures bring hurt to the local congregation they are leading. As Paul said to the church in Colossae, let us "walk in a manner worthy of the Lord, *fully* pleasing to him: bearing fruit in every good work and increasing in the knowledge of God" (Col 1:10; emphasis added). If we do this, we will be well prepared to humbly serve the Lord in the role of elder in our local congregation.

Discussion Questions/Application

1. Why do you think God emphasizes character, and not skill set, as the main focus for qualification for the role of elder in the church?

2. Of the list of character qualifications in 1 Tim 3, Titus 1, and 1 Pet 5, which seems to be the one or two most natural that others have affirmed in your gifting? Which traits are the one or two that are the most challenging?

3. As you examine these traits in your life, what are you willing to do to make these traits real in your life? Who do you need to talk to or what do you need to do to grow in character?

2. *Be Above Reproach*

As MENTIONED ABOVE, ONE of the key areas discussed in that chapter came out of 1 Tim 3 and Titus 1—being "above reproach" (1 Tim 3:2; Titus 1:6). Just to be clear, "above reproach" does not mean sinless or without sin, as no one would be qualified to serve! The concept of "above reproach" does mean that the elder is "above criticism" and no one can easily charge him with wrongdoing. This is such a key area in our battle to keep the highest level of character as an elder. Sadly, it seems that this is an area where men serving as elders are attacked the most by the enemy. We are attacked when we don't have sufficient guidelines in place against the attacks of the devil in our lives. Kevin DeYoung says that an elder "must live a life of Christlike character and virtue that is not easily refuted by those who know him best. The closer you look, the better the mature Christian appears."[1]

In 1 Tim 3:2–7, Paul highlights four key areas in which an overseer should be above reproach: morality, home life, spiritual maturity, and reputation with outsiders. In an age where so much information is available through the Internet, there is far more awareness of the moral failings of pastors. My own senior pastor, Dr. David Jones, has been keeping track of stories related to moral failings over the past seventeen years. He tracks those as a training tool for church planters, as well as a sobering and humbling reminder to himself. Through the accumulation of that data, he is aware of more than 180 evangelical or high-profile pastors who

1. DeYoung, "What Does It Mean," para. 9.

lost their ministries due to a moral failing. Through his research, the most frequent reasons, not surprisingly, for pastoral failing "involve money, sex and/or power."[2]

So, fellow elders, what do we do? Here are a few practical examples of how to be above reproach when it comes to morality:

1. Submit yourself to humble, consistent accountability (Jas 5:16; Heb 3:13)—Be weekly in an accountable relationship with another elder or elder-qualified man. Give that man the permission to ask you any question about your life and walk with the Lord, and vice versa. This should be a consistent practice in your life, preferably weekly if not biweekly.

2. Set up "spiritual guardrails"—A list of four or five things you will do and not do under any circumstances. Give that list to your accountability partner to review at certain times. This list of guardrails is intended to help you stay away from moral failure as you serve the church in the role of elder.

3. Live by the "Billy Graham Rule" with women—Also known as the Modesto Manifesto, these guidelines encourage accountability in money, humility with the local church, and honesty in representing the ministry. However, perhaps the most well-known provision is to not be alone with a woman who is not your wife. This means even when other women may encourage you that it's OK (e.g., a friend asks you to drop off someone's child home from church or another friend asks you to drop something at his house and only that wife is home and she says "feel free to come in," etc.). Follow the principle to avoid any temptation or potential accusation of impropriety.

4. Ensure your character is revealed (Rom 5:3-5; Jas 1:12)— This is the proof of who you really are. Character is the total quality of a person's behavior as revealed in his habits of thought and expression (1 Tim 4:15). Character is revealed by how we treat individuals who can do nothing for us. We

2. David W. Jones, personal communication, June 13, 2023.

must practice the following character-building habits that are spiritual disciplines: quiet time, Scripture memorization, Bible study, evangelism, giving, discipleship, serving, worship, and prayer.

Let's not determine how we engage in the "above reproach" calling in our Christian walks from a worldly perspective, but solely focusing on the word of God. Twenty years ago, a former senior pastor of mine, David Barber, once challenged the men of the church when it came to morality. He said we never want to fall over the cliff, so as men we should keep *plenty* of distance from the edge of the cliff and falling into sin. May that be all the more a goal for us as elders who are called to be "above reproach" (1 Tim 3:2) and "examples to the flock" (1 Pet 5:3). As elders, may we not flirt on the edge of the morality cliff, but run as far away from the edge as possible to serve faithfully and, more importantly, to bring glory to God.

Discussion Questions/Application

1. Humble, consistent accountability can often be a challenge for men. Men are often fiercely independent and don't want to submit to accountability. What has been your experience in submitting to consistent accountability to other men? If you haven't previously had this in your life, are you willing to start now?

2. Why is it essential to enact spiritual guardrails in your life, or, as referenced, the "Billy Graham Rule?" Is this demeaning towards women? Why or why not?

3. Why is living "above reproach" so challenging in today's culture?

4. As you reflect on your own walk with the Lord and what being "above reproach" looks like for you, write down the areas that you'd like to grow in to be "above reproach." This could be in the area of spiritual disciplines, relationship choices,

habits, or life choices. After prayerfully considering that list, provide it to someone that you're willing to submit to in humble accountability.

3. Have Five People in Your Life Who Are Key Friends

WHEN I WAS IN high school, I used to spend a lot of time at Bakers Square, a bygone restaurant chain based in the Midwest. We would meet up there on a Friday night with a big group of our high school friends to have some coffee and pie together. It would typically be anywhere from ten to fifteen people. At the end of the night, it was not uncommon for my dad to ask how the night went. His reaction was always one of dismissiveness and humor when I would tell him the size of the group. I vividly remember him saying, "Someday you'll be able to count the real friends you need on one hand!" Typically, I would counter my dad's challenge with a guffaw based on immaturity and a lack of wisdom. However, my dad was sharing wisdom with me—the critical importance of having a small group of key friends in our lives.

I came to faith in Jesus Christ in college and only now do I realize how much wisdom was in that statement from my dad during my youth. Key relationships in the life of a Christian man lead to accountability, joy, encouragement, and challenge.

If we are to thrive as elders we must not fall away from the vine in our personal sanctification. Jesus said, "I am the vine; you are the branches. Whoever abides in me and I in him, he it is that bears much fruit, for apart from me you can do nothing" (John 15:5). If we operate our Christian life on a spiritual island, we can do nothing.

I believe there are five key people each elder needs in their life to thrive spiritually.

#1&2—A Wise, Godly Couple (If Married)

The enemy is trying to discourage you as an elder, and one of the chief ways he can do that is through your marriage. Identify a wise, godly couple that you know and have them invest in you and your wife's lives. Make a concerted effort to see them consistently together as a couple and have them be part of your life, perhaps once a month. Ensure that couple has influence with you and the capability to ask you hard questions about your life, walk, and ministry.

#3—A Barnabas

Similar to Barnabas's investment in Paul, identify a man of character, elder-qualified, who can invest in your life as you serve as an elder. Give them permission to be able to check in with your spiritual growth, your purity, your walk, and your pursuit of godliness. Whether it is via text, Zoom, or in person, have a consistent check-in time with that brother. In my years as an elder, multiple men served me in this way, and it was truly invaluable.

#4—A Timothy

As we shepherd the flock of God, we need to have a relationship that we are *intentionally* investing in while we serve as an elder. Paul invested in Timothy for many years while he was in the midst of a growing, international mission. We need to guard our hearts as elders and not lose sight of the call to discipleship and mentoring. We should never be too busy to invest in other men. Pray that the Lord would lead you to the right man to invest in at your church. Perhaps it's a young man in the congregation; perhaps it's someone that is new to the elder board; perhaps it's a newer believer. Bottom line—disciple and invest in a "Timothy" in your life.

#5—A Wise, Godly Third-Party Individual (Outside Your Congregation)

This person was incredibly important to me as I served as an elder and, even more so, in serving as a chairman. Unity of the church is very important, and the more we reach out to individuals in our own congregation to get advice or wisdom as we're contemplating something, the higher a possibility of division. That individual may think the board is fragmented or that there are problems.

I had the privilege of serving our local congregation as elder chairman during the COVID years. My wise, godly friend (my "#5") was a ministry leader in a parachurch organization who had experience serving as an elder at a different church. There were several questions that I sought wisdom on that were more appropriate for someone outside the congregation through this tumultuous time, such as:

1. "What do you think my role is versus our senior pastor's in deciding how quickly to move forward in this season of COVID?"

2. "What do you think grace looks like in this season to fellow church members, and how would you suggest I administer that grace?"

3. "Here's how I handled (a particular situation). How would you have handled it?"

4. "How have you been shepherded in your congregation by your elders, and how would you like to be shepherded?"

His answers to these questions and feedback were very helpful in self-evaluation of decision-making and evaluating next steps for leadership.

I found in my years as elder and elder chairman, a key third-party individual was a blessing to have as a sounding board and for encouragement and wisdom as you process through something that may be going on in the church. What are the ideal key characteristics for this individual?

Here are a handful:

1. Elder-qualified (1 Tim 3; Titus 1)

2. Completely trustworthy (Prov 10:9; 11:13)

3. Similar experience (Job 12:12)

4. Not a member of your congregation, preferably, lives some distance away

5. A good listener (Prov 18:13; Jas 1:19)

This outside voice with impartial wisdom has proven to be fruitful not only to me as an elder, but more importantly, in my own walk with the Lord.

Discussion Questions/Application

1. What does prayer have to do with establishing key friendships in your life?

2. In your experience, do Christian men tend to easily form deep friendships? Why or why not? What are ways men can establish deep friendships?

3. Why is it wise for an elder to not only have someone that they are investing in (a Timothy) but also to have someone investing in them (a Barnabas)?

4. Of the list of five key relationships, what do you think is the most critical and why?

5. When thinking of a wise, godly third-party man that can speak into your service as an elder, how do you guard against gossip (Prov 11:13; 16:28; 20:19) in that friendship?

4. *Realize that You're Not a Big Deal*

THE 2004 MOVIE *ANCHORMAN: The Legend of Ron Burgundy* gave a comedic fictional story of news anchor Ron Burgundy. Upon introducing himself to someone at a gathering, he arrogantly stated, "I don't know how to put this, but I'm kind of a big deal. People know me. I'm very important."[1] The individual he was speaking to was not impressed with Burgundy's high level of arrogance. The world tells us that higher levels of leadership are sought after for their prestige, influence, and responsibility. An individual who desires to be an elder/overseer (1 Tim 3:1) should never desire those earthly things and should guard their heart against it.

Elders are, often, the lay leaders responsible for oversight of a local congregation, both legally and doctrinally. With that responsibility comes a weight that you can only understand once you have served as an elder. However, with that leadership responsibility in a local congregation, there can be a temptation that we are "kind of a big deal." People may come to us for answers to questions, practically and theologically. People may come to us with ideas for the church and for ministries. People may come to us with needs for shepherding and care. In and of themselves, none of these are bad things. However, as an elder, do we handle those questions in either an "I'm-kind-of-a-big-deal" or "I'm-not-a-big-deal" way? The difference is substantial and key to how you shepherd. Do a

1. *Anchorman: The Legend of Ron Burgundy*, directed by Adam McKay (Universal City, CA: DreamWorks Pictures, 2004), DVD.

heart check by thinking of situations you've been involved with and assessing the thought process you had in the moment:

"I'm Kind of a Big Deal"—Elder Response

1. What way can I use this to steer the decision to something that's my personal preference or to my benefit?

2. Does this ministry idea line up with my area of interests?

3. Doesn't this person realize I am super busy?

4. I don't have time to go and meet with this person.

5. It's their problem; they got themselves in this situation.

"I'm Not a Big Deal—God Is!"—Elder Response

1. What is God teaching them and me through this situation?

2. Does this question/idea/suggestion line up with the direction God's been calling our congregation?

3. Who's the best person to come alongside and encourage this fellow Christ follower?

4. How can I figure out a way to make time for this person?

5. How can I be transparent with this person to connect and shepherd them?

Consistent humility is key for our own hearts, as well as for those who we are charged with shepherding. Do a heart check on your time serving as an elder, and evaluate which bucket your heart is in. If we are honest, occasionally the enemy tries to get us into the "I'm-kind-of-a-big-deal" bucket, and we must guard our hearts against that temptation.

Jesus told his own disciples that "if anyone would come after me, let him deny himself and take up his cross daily and follow me" (Luke 9:23). Elders—we have to remind ourselves that our service in the church is countercultural. We are not to think highly of ourselves (Rom 12:3; 1 Cor 4:7) in our role, but we should be the chief example of denying ourselves and serving others (Mark 10:45). Our role as elders is all for God's glory (1 Cor 10:31) and not our own (Ps 115:1). We should be pointing our finger not at ourselves and our importance but to the goodness of God in our lives each and every day.

Discussion Questions/Application

1. Do a heart check evaluation. As you read through the list of "I'm-kind-of-a-big-deal" responses, were there any you resonated with or experienced in the past?

2. Why is humility such an important part of being an elder?

3. The world emphasizes specific traits in effective leaders. Some of these traits may include a commanding presence, arrogance, and being a good speaker and manager. How can an elder who is humble, and vastly different than these earthly traits, still be an effective servant leader in the church?

5. *Prioritize Your Wife and Family*

THE BEST THING THAT ever happened to me was crossing paths with my wife at the age of nineteen. We were in campus ministry together, and we actually didn't really like each other at all. We didn't get along. Seriously. The less mature, younger version of myself was so blind as a new Christian to the blessing God had put before me. I'm thankful that changed!

Our wives and families are a priority when we serve the church as a shepherd. This is not only because they are our most important responsibility on earth, but also because God commands it of elders "He must manage his own household well, with all dignity keeping his children submissive, for if someone does not know how to manage his own household, how will he care for God's church?" (1 Tim 3:4–5)

My wife has been integrally involved in my serving as an elder. In fact, the decision to serve as an elder is a decision for both the husband and wife to make *together*. The simple fact is that much weight also falls on her shoulders. If you have young children, she may have to carry extra weight when a shepherding crisis occurs. Additionally, spouses can sometimes feel the weight of being the "elder's wife." Some examples of that weight can look like expectations to be at certain events or knowledge of a difficult relational situation in the church that she needs to keep confidential. Encourage her in this season of service through consistently showing your appreciation of her for partnering with you in ministry. Prioritize date nights with her where the focus of your discussion is not on the ministry of the church but on what she wants to discuss. In your years of service to the church, there will be seasons when your wife needs more of your attention. In younger years of marriage, this may be due to the physical weariness of child-rearing. As you mature in your marriage, that may be because of the emotional weariness of your young adults moving into adulthood, or perhaps grief she's experiencing. We must be in touch with our spouses so we can serve them in those seasons of transition. Make sure that we are allowing space for our wives to share their frustrations and concerns.

I remember my first three years serving as an elder were particularly difficult. When the time for renewal for another term came up, I was convicted that my wife and I were going to pray about serving and if she said she couldn't do it for another term, I was going to step down. Much to my surprise, after prayer, she said, "I think we should serve for another term." I needed to give her the space to process and know that she was a key, if not *the* key, to that decision. Brothers, love your wives (Eph 5:25; Col 3:19; 1 Pet 3:7). One of the ways the enemy will attack an elder is to cause problems between his wife and him. This will hinder your walk with the Lord and your prayer life (1 Pet 3:7). Don't rush your wife along, as I have been convicted of doing far too many times over the years. Be aware that the enemy will try to get you offtrack. It's vitally important that you "live with your wife in an understanding way" (1 Pet 3:7).

I encourage you, fellow elder, to love your children well during the season of serving. For elders who still have children in the home, your children already watch your every move as a parent. How much more will they be watching to see how you serve his church! If you have young children in the home, your children will be learning from you what it's like to serve with a joyful heart. They will be learning from you where they fall in the prioritization hierarchy. Here are a few things I discovered from my years of raising children while serving as an elder.

Intentionally Disciple Them, Individually

Have a weekly scheduled time with each of your children to disciple them individually. Have ears to listen to them, ask how they're doing, and walk them through the building blocks of being a Christian man or woman. Teach them how to share the gospel, emphasize the importance of serving the Lord, memorize Scripture with them, and encourage them to live a life of accountability. We need to teach them how to engage in the culture and respond to the times in a sound, biblical manner. Not only are all of these a spiritual investment in each of them, it's a great way to bond with your children.

Find Ways You Can Serve with Them

If our children see our service as an elder as a "church thing" and a "thing Dad does" and they are not part of it, we have failed. Find ways to serve together with your sons and daughters. Perhaps that's part of the set-up or clean-up at the men's breakfast. Perhaps that's singing in the choir together for Easter with your daughter. Perhaps that's making and delivering a meal together for a family in need or struggling. Seek the Lord and find ways you can serve together.

Joyful Service as Part of Your Identity in Christ

Our children should see that service is not an option for us, but it is a natural outcome of our love for Jesus Christ. "As each has received a gift, use it to serve one another, as good stewards of God's varied grace" (1 Pet 3:10). We have been gifted by the Lord. Our children should see that we're more than willing to do any task to serve others. Our culture might imbue in us that we are a big deal and others should serve us. However, Christ did not come to be served, but to serve (Mark 10:45). Pray and check your heart before you serve. Ensure that your children are seeing your service as the natural and joyful overflow of your heart (Luke 6:45) for what God did for us in Christ Jesus.

Discussion Questions/Application

1. Why do you think wives feel the weight of being "an elder's wife?" What is it about the church that puts that stress on them? How can we come alongside our wives and encourage them in this area?

2. What do you think are some ideas or effective ways to include your wife in your ministry as an elder?

3. If you have children at home, take time to jot down thoughts on how you can intentionally invest in them while you serve as an elder. Discuss that list with your wife and come up with a plan to set aside and prioritize time for discipling and investing in your children.

4. Does your wife feel that she can share with you about how your marriage is going in the season of serving as an elder? Do you have an established time to check in with her and see how she's flourishing during that season? Take time to discuss this with your wife and come up with a plan.

6. *Guard Against Earthly Wisdom; Strive for Godly Wisdom*

WHEN GOD CALLS MEN to serve in the role of elder, we strive for godly wisdom. However, when the world starts to encroach on us as we serve, there can be a temptation to transition and start using earthly wisdom.

What's the difference between the two? The Bible is quite clear in contrasting earthly and godly wisdom in Jas 3:13–17.

Characteristics of Earthly Wisdom	Characteristics of Godly Wisdom
• Bitter jealousy (v14)	• Good conduct (v13)
• Selfish ambition (v14)	• Meekness (v13)
• Disorder (v16)	• Pure (v17)
• Vile practices (v16)	• Peaceable (v17)
• Demonic (v15)	• Gentle (v17)
• Unspiritual (v15)	• Open to reason (v17)
	• Full of mercy (v17)
	• Full of good fruits (v17)
	• Impartial (v17)
	• Sincere (v17)

In making decisions and seeking wisdom, we have to do some heart analysis to assess what the motivation is for our wisdom and decision-making. I would propose asking some of the following heart-check questions to assess if you are working in earthly wisdom or godly wisdom:

1. Am I trying to address my personal desires or submit to God?

2. Am I trying to make the recipient happy and be at peace with them, or am I telling them what God's calling me to share?

3. Am I centering my thoughts/wisdom on the word of God or on some tradition that I'm used to because that is how we've always done it? Can I point to Scripture supporting the wisdom that is on my heart and mind?

4. Are my thoughts/opinions based on me having a vested interest, or do I stand to benefit from it? Is it to make me look good, or am I making the decision based on bringing God glory?

5. Have godly men, whom I respect, given their thoughts on the topic? Does it biblically line up with my thoughts?

Some years, ago, I had a friend who was going through a difficult season of marriage for eight to ten years. His wife was struggling with severe alcoholism and would not get help. It was affecting his marriage and their child. He was exhausted and wanted to get a divorce. He came to me, as an elder, for advice and counsel. By listening to him, I understood he was looking for a stamp of approval on his decision to divorce. In conversation, I also heard from him there was no unfaithfulness (Matt 5:32), abandonment (1 Cor 7:13–15), or physical abuse (1 Cor 7:15). He was just, understandably, tired of dealing with the marriage and the struggles. Earthly wisdom, as a friend, would have told him that I felt sorry for him and understood his decision. The world would totally accept the reasons for his divorce. Earthly wisdom would be that he should do what was best for himself. However, a Christ follower's litmus test is different. Therefore, godly wisdom was required to challenge him that he didn't have biblical grounds for divorce and he would not, biblically, be allowed to remarry (Matt 5:31–32). I explained that God was teaching both he and his wife something through this experience and struggle. Sadly, he still decided to divorce his wife, and it turned into an ugly, drawn-out divorce battle. Although that was not the outcome I had hoped for and desired based on the Scriptures, I trust that God will honor the sharing of his word (Isa 55:11) and accomplish what he wants with it in his time, not in my time.

Modern culture encourages us to make decisions based on our feelings and what makes us happy rather than what is wise. In an age of social media, there is tremendous encouragement of self-help and narcissistic decision-making based on what makes an individual happy, regardless of godly wisdom.

May we not be distracted by the subtle inculcation of worldly ideas and thoughts that our culture endlessly impresses upon us. Fellow elders, let us be men of the word of God. In your walk as an elder, strive for godly wisdom and "hold firm to the trustworthy word" (Titus 1:9). We are called to that in our role.

Discussion Questions/Application

1. When reading through the list of godly and earthly wisdom from Jas 3, what stood out to you and why?

2. Which of the heart-check questions spoke to you most vibrantly and why?

3. In serving as an elder, what are the most effective ways to keep the focus of our heart on godly wisdom instead of earthly wisdom?

4. Why do we have to guard against making decisions based on what makes us happy or based on our feelings? Consider Jer 17:9 and Prov 14:12–13.

7. Steward Your Resources

IN THE LIST OF character qualifications for "the office of overseer (elder)" (1 Tim 3:1) is the following—"not a lover of money" (1 Tim 3:3). As part of our personal sanctification, we need to develop the discipline not to be a lover of money. If we are managing our finances in a biblical manner, this is not something that the congregation will see. Your spouse and the Lord will be the primary observers of this discipline of not loving money. However, it is critical for your role as elder and for your own personal sanctification growth.

How can we be sure that we are stewarding our resources well and we are not lovers of money?

Pray for the Lord's Guidance—Use the Tithe as Baseline

The Old Testament prescribed a few different offerings: (A) the Levitical tithe which was 10 percent (Lev 27:30–33; Num 18:21–24), (B) the tithe of the Feasts which was 10 percent (Deut 14:22–27), and (C) the benevolence tithe for the poor which was 10 percent every three years (Deut 14:28–29). Essentially, this adds up to 23.3 percent per year. The New Testament encourages cheerful giving and does not prescribe a specific amount to give. We are managing God's money and called to cheerfully give. While 10 percent is a good baseline to start with, make sure that you are giving in a manner that is prayerfully considered and consistent with cheerful giving (2 Cor 9:7).

Keep an Emergency Jubilee/Blessing Fund

There are needs that always arise in the life of a church. Separate from your tithe giving, set some money to the side that you have saved for emergencies that arise so you may bless somebody in need. One idea is to set aside the same amount you are using for weekly incidental spending (coffee out, lunch out, etc.). When a need arises, pray about it and give generously and anonymously (Matt 6:3–4). Here is one way you can accomplish this task: Write an encouraging, type-written note of what the Lord has done in your life and give it to someone with a gift. Share that you were convicted to be a blessing to the person in need. Place that in an envelope with the individual's name on it. Enclose that envelope inside of *another* envelope that you can give to a trusted, close friend. Then, ask your friend to give it to someone else they trust (a separate third party) and to open the envelope after the friend leaves. Have them explain to the third party that they received this gift from someone who wishes to remain anonymous and were asked to give it to a third party to deliver it. All the glory goes to the Lord through that anonymous giving.

Heart-Check Questions to Ask Yourself as You Make Financial Decisions

There is wisdom in asking some heart-check questions when it comes to finances to determine if you are a lover of money. Consistently ask yourself some of the following questions to assess your heart as it relates to the love of money and stewarding resources:

1. Do you love God more than money and what other people think of you?

2. Am I giving to impress other people (Matt 6:2–4; Prov 3:9) or to honor the Lord, cheerfully (2 Cor 9:7)?

3. Are you content with what God has provided for your family?

4. How often do you check your bank accounts or retirement accounts and think about finances?

5. Am I jealous of other individuals' possessions?

6. Do I seek after friends who are wealthy?

7. Am I in credit card debt? If so, why?

8. Is my giving affected by the purchases I make?

These are just a few ways to do a consistent heart check on stewarding resources. God calls us not to be a lover of money and much of that work is between us and the Lord. How are we to steward the church's funds if we can't steward our own funds well? Fellow elder, let's lean into godly stewardship on a consistent basis.

Discussion Questions/Application

1. When you think and evaluate your own giving, is it often out of obligation, willingness, or both?

2. What is the most challenging part of being a consistent giver as a discipline?

3. In reading through the heart-check questions on stewardship, were there specific ones that stood out to you as challenging and, if so, why did those stand out?

4. Take an evaluation of your own stewardship and tithe giving with your wife. List out the ways that you currently invest God's resources for his purposes. Prayerfully consider if God is calling you to stay the course or make some changes in your cheerful giving (2 Cor 9:7).

Part II—A Shepherd's Work: Shepherding the Flock

8. *Keep the Main Thing the Main Thing*

INDEED.COM IS ONE OF the largest job databases in the United States with more than 250 million users.[1] Indeed recently described a board member's role as follows:

> The purpose of a board of directors includes developing an organization's policies, strategizing ways to meet goals, ensuring that operations abide by relevant laws and regulations and making sure that any decisions or actions align with the interests of all stakeholders.[2]

I conducted a recent search on Amazon for certain leadership-related topics. Here are the number of books that were available for these particular keyword searches:

- Christian Leadership—2,661
- Elder Leadership—138
- Shepherding—118

Our culture clearly has a keen interest on the topic of leadership. Within the church, that interest is in Christian leadership and how a Christ follower should lead. Much of that leadership can, and should, be influenced by the Bible. However, Christian leadership can also can be influenced by the culture.

I completely agree those are *some* of the responsibilities of an elder board. However, too often that list of elder responsibilities

1. Jennings, "Best Job Site," para. 6.
2. Indeed, "Board of Director Title," para. 5.

stops at a church, whether implicitly or practically. If left there, the elder board becomes simply an administrative function to strategize on growing the church and obtaining statistical success. We are not running a business; we are shepherding the body of Christ (Rom 12:5).

We need to remind ourselves afresh of the exhortation in 1 Pet 5 to willingly "shepherd the flock of God that is among you (us)" (1 Pet 5:2). Be engaged in and known for shepherding your congregation. This applies to both the extroverts and the introverts on the elder board! Men, being hospitable (1 Tim 3:2) goes far beyond just inviting people over to our homes. It is truly loving and caring for God's people! This is a quality that is often overlooked, and to be an elder you must love people!

Here are some good heart checks to see if we are focusing enough time on shepherding as an elder:

1. What is the allocation of time spent in our elder meetings on metrics and strategy versus shepherding the flock?

2. Do we have our congregations divided among the elders in an efficient matter to ensure that they are shepherded well by our elders and pastors? Do we hold each other accountable to that shepherding?

3. Are we known to the congregation by name and face through investment in their lives, or are we just known by being on the website and occasionally seen? Are we available to pray with people after services and answer questions? Are we approachable to the congregation outside of services?

4. Do we spend our extra time outside of the meetings striving to shepherd those in our congregations through struggles they are experiencing?

5. What motivates you more: growth in church attendance or seeing congregants repent and put their faith in Jesus Christ?

There are several factors that impact the job responsibilities of a shepherding elder at a church: the size and demographics of the congregation, cultural setting, and the quantity of staff members, to name a few. However, as elders, the exhortation across *any* congregation is we are specifically called to shepherd the flock of God! May we be brave shepherds to our congregations, speak truth (Titus 1:9; Eph 4:15), and do it well to the praise of his glorious grace (Eph 1:6) and for the benefit of the church.

Discussion Questions/Application

1. What do you think are the main ways that church leadership/ elder boards are influenced by cultural wisdom? Are those all bad or can some of that influence be positive?

2. "Shepherding the flock" is a key focus of an elder (1 Pet 5). Discuss the many different ways that an elder board can effectively shepherd a congregation.

3. If you're currently serving as an elder, does your elder board spend a sufficient amount of time and ministerial energy on shepherding the flock? Why or why not?

4. In order to effectively shepherd the flock of God, the sheep (congregation) need to know who the elders are at a church. Discuss effective ways to make yourself available, as a shepherd elder, in order to grow in connecting with the sheep (congregants) at your local congregation.

9. *If You Give a Yard, Be Willing to Go a Mile*

IN *A SHEPHERD'S LOOK at Psalm 23* Phillip Keller describes a shepherd's protection of his sheep from various pests. Keller describes how sheep cannot sit still in the summer as they're bothered by flies and bugs so they are always moving around. Keller writes the following:

> Only the diligent care of the owner who keeps a constant lookout for these insects will prevent them from annoying his flock. . . . This all entails considerable extra care. It takes time and labor and expensive chemicals to do the job thoroughly. It means, too, that the sheepman must be amongst his charges daily, keeping a close watch on their behavior. As soon as there is the least evidence that they are being disturbed he must take steps to provide them with relief. Always uppermost in his mind is the aim of keeping his flock quiet, contented and at peace.[1]

Keller highlights that "diligent care" and "constant lookout" is required to properly care for the flock. Shepherding the flock is hard. In a Western culture that wants quick results, shepherding is not like that. It requires patience and diligence. Perhaps your congregation has a couple in the throes of a collapsing marriage, another that is struggling with habitual lying, and yet a third is struggling with pornography. These are struggles that are

---

1. Keller, *Shepherd Looks*, 38.

preventing them from flourishing and resting in peace before the Lord. These are not quick-fix shepherding assignments.

As elders, we must remind ourselves that many times, people are stuck in their sin and unwilling to receive shepherding and care. However, when people are willing to repent and work on their struggle(s) and give us a "yard" of effort, we need to be prepared to, figuratively, go a mile to shepherd them. I see three charges God provides to elders to not only go a yard, but to go a full mile in shepherding.

Willingly Provide Shepherding

We have to go beyond expectation and beyond obligation. We must "willingly" (1 Pet 5:2) and "eagerly" (1 Pet 5:4) shepherd the flock. Joyfully follow up with individuals and meet with them, incorporate others that have that area of expertise, and send encouraging Scriptures. The members in your care should know that you love them and that you are there for them.

Lean In! It's a Spiritual Battle

This battle against sin is against the "cosmic powers over this present darkness, against the spiritual forces of evil in the heavenly places" (Eph 6:12). Our enemy, the devil, is consistently trying to discourage and distract us from the things of God. May we have the courage and perseverance to encourage someone with the truths of Scripture to win the victory over sin. We are called as elders to "rebuke" (Titus 1:9) false doctrines and as "older men" (Titus 2:2) to challenge younger men with sound doctrine (Titus 2:1). If one of your sheep starts to stray, lean in again. The path to victory over sin is less of a linear increase and more of a cosine curve with *ups and downs* increasing over time:

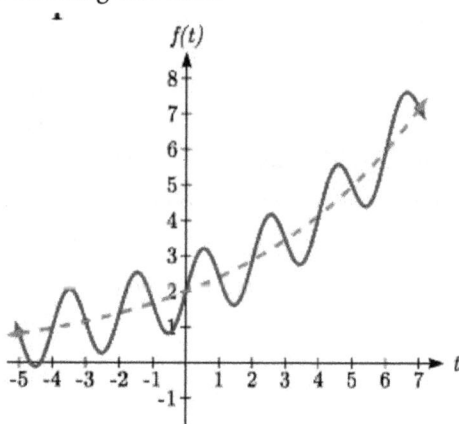

Be a Witness to Others, Go the Extra Mile

We live in a culture that gets frustrated if shipping takes more than two to three days to be delivered. Everything has to be fast. If we go beyond expectations and show commitment to struggling sheep, it makes nonbelievers ask why we went the extra mile. That extra mile can be a prayer and shepherding investment for a week, months, or years. The world is watching, and that extra love for a brother or sister in Christ is a testimony that we are Christ's disciples (John 13:35). Elder, that extra care, effort, and love to encourage victory over sin is one of the many ways the church can differentiate itself from the world. Be willing to go the extra mile!

Discussion Questions/Application

1. Discuss ways that you can practically, and effectively, "go the extra mile" to shepherd those in your congregation.

2. Peter emphasizes in 1 Peter the importance of elders shepherding "eagerly" and "willingly." How do you think an elder evaluates if his shepherding is done reluctantly or unwillingly?

3. Discuss how maintaining vibrant and consistent shepherding of the congregation can be a witness to a watching world. Provide examples, if you have them.

4. As mentioned, our culture emphasizes efficiency and values fast completion of everything. Often times, however, shepherding congregants through a situation will not be completed quickly. How can an elder communicate those time expectations, as it relates to shepherding a situation, to an individual in the flock?

10. *Be OK with Releasing People*

SCRIPTURE IS CLEAR THAT we are called to diligently pursue those in our congregations (1 Pet 5:2). We are also to come alongside those who are struggling with sin. Shepherding often includes pursuing those in our congregation who are currently struggling with apathy toward the Lord.

However, how do we shepherd if an individual continues to ignore our challenges to turn from sin? How do we react if the individual fails to take their faith walk seriously, repent, and turn toward Christ?

I was meeting with a young man a few years back in a discipleship relationship. The first several months went great. However, at that point there was a change in his commitment. He consistently showed up with an incomplete discipleship workbook. He consistently gave blasé answers to our discussion topics. As I shared this struggle with a wise and respected brother in Christ in my life he said, "You need to release him and let the Lord work in his life." What? Release him? No, that can't be correct, I thought. I simply need a different strategy or a different approach and surely that will encourage him to focus on his walk with Christ (or so I thought). With some reluctance, I met with this young man and said that I thought it would be best for us to stop meeting until he was at a place in life where he could commit to our plans, but I'd be available when he was at a place in his life to intentionally invest in growing in his love and obedience to Jesus Christ.

Fast forward about eighteen months, this young man showed up at my office, unannounced. He said he needed to talk with me and what he shared was beyond humbling. He said releasing him was the best thing I could have done in shepherding him. He confessed using me as a crutch to "faith," and the Lord needed to do a work in his life, which needed to be done without me.

As overseers for the church, we are called to shepherd the flock, but we also need to steward our time well. Paul, in his letter to the Ephesians, stated, "Look carefully then how you walk, not as unwise but as wise, making the best use of the time, because the days are evil" (Eph 5:15–16).

Here are some practical ways to assess when it is time to release someone we are shepherding and how to effectively and lovingly release them:

When?

1. Have we met with an individual four to five times to discuss his struggle/current faithlessness without much active change in their life?

2. Do we want them to change more than they want to change?

3. Do we find ourselves coming up with unbiblical rationales as to why the person continues to ignore the challenge to re-engage in their walk with Christ?

4. Have we worked with this individual and sought the wisdom of bringing someone else into the situation (Matt 18:16) and seen no change?

5. As an overseer, are we ignoring new shepherding opportunities to continue to meet with particular individuals, yet not seeing any movement toward improvement on the congregant's part?

If the answer to these questions is "yes," it might be time to lovingly release him to the Lord for him to work in his life.

How?

1. Pray for the Lord to give wisdom in the conversation.

2. Ask to meet with the individual, in person.

3. Affirm the individual and lovingly discuss what you have tried to do to shepherd them and encourage them.

4. Discuss with the individual whether there has been consistent fruit seen as a result of the shepherding relationship.

5. Discuss the Scriptures associated with stewardship of time (e.g., Ps 90:12; Eph 5:15–16; Col 1:10).

6. Encourage them to fervently seek the Lord through the Scriptures.

7. Affirm to them that when there is a genuine change in the situation toward Christ, you or another elder would be more than willing to provide wisdom on next steps.

Fellow elder, we love God's people, but we need to ensure that we are following the Lord's leading by the power of the Holy Spirit and stewarding our time well!

Discussion Questions/Application

1. What is the hardest part about releasing someone you are shepherding?

2. In reviewing the list of evaluation questions for when to release someone from shepherding, what from the list do you agree with the most and which one from the list do you disagree with, and why?

3. Let's review the list of how to release someone from shepherding. What seems the most natural to you and what do you think would be the most challenging for you?

11. *Shepherd the "Confident" Because They Are Probably Hurting*

MOST LIKELY, EVERY ELDER has encountered "Charlie Confidence" at their church. Charlie comes across as very knowledgeable (on many topics). He is happy to quickly point out what has been going wrong in the church services recently or to share specific details of a sermon that could have been delivered better. Charlie will sometimes "stir the pot" because he portrays confidence to those around him and people are willing to listen.

As an elder chairman, I always encourage my fellow shepherds to engage with the "Charlie Confidences" in the congregation. The reason is that these individuals may seem confident, but they are often hurting or very insecure.

Some years back there was a member of our congregation who wanted to meet with me, as an elder, to discuss issues he had with our pastor's sermons. After quite literally two and a half hours straight of ranting about ten to fifteen specific sermons, he claimed our pastor had contradicted the Bible over the past two years. I calmly said I did not remember those particular instances. I did commit, however, to go back and listen to all of those sermons and review the accusations. However, as I was praying in that moment on how to end the conversation, the Lord revealed to me to ask him how his marriage was going.

What? I thought, *Where did that come from?*

41

At that moment, I trusted in the Lord's leading, looked the individual in the eyes, and asked the question: "Hey, how is your marriage going?"

Game changer.

As it turned out, the issues presented about the sermons and church were just a smokescreen covering a hurting brother in Christ whose marriage was falling apart. Suddenly, the allegations and rants were a distant memory, and we had a discussion on steps to take in order to repair a broken marriage. He transitioned from a combative congregant to a hurting brother.

Do not be intimidated by an arrogant or ranting member of your congregation. Pray for them and shepherd them! Lovingly encourage them to pursue humility. Pastor Josh Squires states, "Pride is a prison that perpetuates anger, hurt, and foolishness while keeping at bay the restorative effects of conviction, humility and reconciliation."[1] How true!

We are in a spiritual battle. Let us remind ourselves that those difficult congregants who are struggling with arrogance or pride and are challenging to us as elders may be deeply hurting. Let us be brave enough as overseers to encourage them to break out of that "prison"[2] so they find the joy of "humility and reconciliation."[3]

Discussion Questions/Application

1. Why do you think that some of the most confident individuals are the most in need of elder shepherding?

2. Often times the confident, or perhaps even arrogant, individuals in our congregation can be intimidating to other members of the congregation and even the pastoral staff. As an elder, how do you go about engaging and shepherding those individuals that come across as arrogant or intimidating to others?

1. Squires, "Pride Is Your Greatest Problem," para. 4.
2. Squires, "Pride Is Your Greatest Problem," para. 4.
3. Squires, "Pride Is Your Greatest Problem," para. 4.

3. Discuss how prayer is critical to these shepherding relation-ships. If you have practical examples of how prayer has im-pacted difficult shepherding relationships, feel free to share.

12. *Often the Thing That's the Thing, Is Not the Thing*

THE OLD SAYING GOES, "You don't know what you don't know!" When the Lord called me to be an elder over a decade ago, I appreciated that a solid brother in Christ asked me some hard questions to evaluate if I was ready to be an elder. He asked things I had not thought through completely:

1. Do you *love* the church and want to see it be healthy and unified?

2. Do you *love* the people of the church and want to see them be sanctified?

Those were truly great questions to evaluate before going into the role of elder. I answered "yes" that day to both of those questions. However, little did I know how difficult that second question would be at times.

One of the things I would encourage you, fellow elder, is to be aware and mindful how pride voraciously infiltrates the church and makes shepherding challenging. I love the definition Merriam-Webster's dictionary provides for pride: "exaggerated self-esteem."[1]

When I say "often the thing that's the thing, is not the thing," the shepherding challenge is often breaking through pride in someone's life. We will often be asked to shepherd someone through a situation; however, the Holy Spirit reveals to us through that

1. Merriam-Webster, "Pride."

interaction that the real issue they are having has nothing to do with the original topic. Here are some real shepherding examples (names have been changed for anonymity) I have had in my years as elder, and perhaps you can identify with some of them:

The "thing" the church member originally wanted to discuss with an elder	What was actually going on in their life?	How did we get there?
John and Joan ask to talk about the frustration they've been having with the way that the pastor hasn't been using personal applications in the sermon.	Their personal devotional life was extremely dry, and the marriage was struggling.	Prayed and asked questions during the meeting such as, "What is going well and what's not going well right now in your marriage?"
Bob comes to the front of the church after service and wants to talk about the men's breakfast from this past Saturday.	The Lord used the message from the breakfast to impact his life. He wanted to share it with someone but was intimidated to have a deep, personal discussion.	Prayed and asked Bob, "How has God been speaking to you and revealing himself in your life recently?"
Pastor Tom sets up a meeting with me to go over some ideas he had related to the missions committee.	Pastor Tom was feeling lonely and discouraged through various interpersonal struggles he has had with the mission team. However, he didn't want to come across as weak and struggling.	Prayed and asked Pastor Tom, "Before we get started, can you share with me what is going well and what is not going well in your life right now?"

You see, brothers, to encourage our flock, we need *discernment*. By the power of the Holy Spirit, we must discern what "the thing" is that's actually going on in someone's life. How can we do this effectively as an elder?

1. Pray and ask the Lord for discernment and clarity.

2. Emphasize personal prayer. Pray continuously over the situation (Rom 12:12; 1 Thess 5:17).

3. Be a great listener. Be quick to hear and slow to speak, and don't answer until you first listen (Jas 1:19; Prov 18:13).

4. Be a question asker. Ask a lot of good questions. Jesus asked hundreds of questions throughout the Gospels; however, he directly answered very few questions that were posed to him. Jesus was the master at asking questions to reveal the current state of a person's heart. He is God and knows all things (Col 1:17).

We must be very careful as elders to listen and understand before we speak or give counsel. Pray for the Lord to give you discernment through the above steps; to break through pride, ascertain the true "thing" someone is dealing with, and shepherd him well through it.

Discussion Questions/Application

1. Why do you think it is often the case that someone's actual struggle is not clearly evident when shepherding them?

2. When shepherding someone to evaluate what the "thing" is that's going on in their life, the chapter discussed the importance of praying, listening, and asking questions. Are any of those more important in the process, and if so, why?

3. In your own personal shepherding of the flock, which of the following is the most challenging: praying for the situation or individual, listening to the sheep, or asking questions of them? Why?

13. *Address Unexpected Issues and Continue Moving Forward*

I LIVE IN AN area where there are a lot of trees and open space. We see all sorts of animals traversing our property: deer, geese, foxes, coyotes, and squirrels, just to name a few. We also have rabbits. When a rabbit goes running across the property, it is common for it to jut toward the left at full speed for ten feet, then turn forty-five degrees to the right for another ten feet . . . and the cycle continues to repeat.

It has been my experience that, as elders, when we sense the Lord moving us in a direction as a church, an unexpected issue often arises. It could be a discussion about a personal preference item at the church, a spiritual attack of some sort against a pastor or one of the leaders, or a rumor about the church. I remember during a significantly difficult season in the life of our church I was part of the team working on revising our constitution. In this same season, my wife and I were embroiled in two difficult relational situations that were taking an undue amount of time from both of us. It was frustrating, emotional, and distracting. However, what I quickly realized was this was a rabbit trail by the enemy. While these rabbit trails are often important and definitely should be addressed and require shepherding, they should not completely take us off the overarching direction the Lord has provided the church leadership. My experience has been that these often arise when the elders sense the Lord moving in a new or revised direction.

Nehemiah 6 is a perfect example of a "rabbit trail" and how the enemy tries to distract us. Nehemiah was called to rebuild the wall around Jerusalem, and the enemy tried to get him off course multiple times. Sanballat and others jeered (Neh 2:19; 4:1) at the Israelites. They even tried to form an army to battle the Israelites. However, Nehemiah didn't waver in his calling. Laborers building the wall were working with "one hand and held [their] weapon with the other" (Neh 4:17). Nehemiah persevered despite distractions and opposition, finishing the wall in fifty-two days, and all nations around them acknowledged that the work was "accomplished with the help of our God" (Neh 6:16). Nehemiah was a godly leader who focused on God's calling and did not chase rabbit trails. As a servant leader, he was a wise steward of time and resources.

My encouragement, brothers, is when the elders have consensus over a particular direction as a church, have your spiritual discernment "antennas" up as you work to implement that direction. Watch out for distractions and rabbit trails, and be leery of how much time they are pulling you away from the mission the Lord has provided you.

If one of those rabbit trails pop up or the enemy is taking you off course through a distraction, here are things to pursue and things to avoid when addressing the matter:

Pursue	Avoid
Commit the matter to prayer.	Reacting and chasing down the issue immediately.
Continue to pursue the strategy/ vision the Lord laid on the elder board's heart.	Consuming a lot of time of your elder meetings on the "rabbit trail" topic.
If necessary, assign one to two elders to lean into the situation as a "subcommittee" and report back to the board.	All of the elders chiming in at board meetings on these topics.
Keep the strategic goals of the church in the forefront of your meeting and pursue them.	Letting the flavor of the day distraction/topic be the main focus of your elder board.

Our enemy who "prowls around like a roaring lion" (1 Pet 5:8), would like nothing more than to take the leadership of the church off course. We must be aware of the tactics of our enemy so "we [are] not outwitted by Satan; for we are not ignorant of his designs" (2 Cor 2:11). As strategic and prowling as the enemy is in trying to have us chase rabbit trails, we need to be even more focused in our charge to discern the Lord's will and fervently shepherd the flock entrusted to us.

Discussion Questions/Application

1. The chapter talked about the concept of "rabbit trails" in ministry. Why do you think those come up during critical moments of ministry?

2. When "rabbit trails" are presented before us, should they all be ignored? Are some of them good for the ministry?

3. If you sense the elder board is being distracted by a "rabbit trail," how can you respectfully address it with the group while still working towards unity as a group?

14. *Avoid Rushing, God's Timing Is Perfect*

I AM A HUGE basketball and NBA fan. Recently, I was watching the replay results from the prior evening and discovered something interesting. The Memphis Grizzlies were up by eight points on the Brooklyn Nets with 4:23 to go in the game. After the Nets made a basket to cut it to six, Memphis forward Santi Adalma slowly rolled the ball in bounds. Memphis Grizzlies superstar Ja Morant feigned that he was going to pick up the ball, but let it roll without touching it. You see, according to the rules, the twenty-four-second shot clock does not start until somebody touches the ball. The Nets didn't guard him and Morant patiently waited until the ball gently rolled over the half-court line, and somebody approached him, then picked it up . . . after twenty-one seconds had elapsed from the clock. Morant just turned a twenty-four-second shot clock into, essentially, a forty-five-second shot clock. Brooklyn was thrown off by the move, did not score for another two minutes, and lost the game to Memphis 134–124. Morant understood the game and was patient with the clock.

As elders we are definitely not playing a game. We are entrusted with a serious responsibility. Shepherding our congregations requires a steady hand led by the wisdom and power of the Holy Spirit. But similar to Ja Morant's serious understanding of the game, we have to know and understand our churches, patiently shepherd them, and not rush anything. God guides men, leaders, and elders. Satan rushes them. We rarely have to make quick decisions.

"Desire without knowledge is not good, and whoever makes haste with his feet misses his way" (Prov 19:2). Men, we desire to see our churches flourish spiritually, numerically, missionally, etc. However, just because something seems good on paper doesn't mean that the Lord wants us to rush and pursue it. Here are some real examples:

1. Somebody is giving your ministry a wonderful gift of monetary value in the form of a parsonage building, but the donors have specific stipulations on how it's to be used, which are extensive (walls you can't paint, who is allowed to live there, etc.). The church is struggling financially, so hastily you accept the gift and are appreciative. However, come to find out over the next three to five years that stewarding the gift of that building with its stipulations is a huge distraction from the mission and vision of the church and takes a tremendous number of staff hours, so you eventually sell the building.

2. A local church plant, currently meeting in a school, had the opportunity to try and purchase a former commercial building on a main road ten minutes away. Perfect location—yes. Street frontage—yes. After pursuit, prayer, and consideration of various legal matters, the church discerned it was not what the Lord was calling them to do. Within a short time frame, one of their church leaders contacted them and wanted to sell them a significant plot of land at a substantial discount, a much better fit for that congregation.

In the first example, a hasty decision was made. They didn't let the ball slowly roll down the court. Hasty decisions are very often wrong decisions. That hasty decision led to years of figuring out how to make the congregant happy, honor their gift, and yet keep the church on mission. In the second example, they did not rush and God gave them what was needed in his timing.

What is my advice for how to avoid rushing things and waiting on God's timing? My friend Dave Corning, chairman of Entrusted

Ministries, likes to explain it this way. He often says, "I can tell you what God's will is for your life." When people shockingly say, "Huh?," he answers with the following from 1 Thess 5: "'Rejoice always, pray without ceasing, give thanks in all circumstances; *for this is the will of God in Jesus Christ for you*'" (1 Thess 5:16–18; emphasis added).

Take time to pray over all decisions and shepherding counsel, even the little moments. While this may seem obvious, I'm sure you and I have both been guilty of hastily making decisions without praying and seeking the counsel of many (Prov 15:22), along with the plurality of elders (Acts 14:23; 16:4; 20:17; 21:18; Titus 1:5; Jas 5:14).

When your church is provided a unique opportunity from the Lord, it might just be unbelievable or shocking how the Lord seems to be providing. However, do not rush into next steps blindly without praying and seeking the Lord and discerning wisdom from the counsel of many elders.

Discussion Questions/Application

1. Why do we have a tendency to want to rush decisions instead of waiting for the Lord?

2. What are some practical and tactical things you can do as an elder to avoid rushing decisions?

3. Is there a risk that, in trying to avoid rushing a decision, an elder board can get caught in a paralysis of analysis? How can you find the right balance? Consider the following Scriptures in your answer: 1 Thess 5:16–18; Ps 119:105; Jas 1:5; Prov 15:22.

15. *Be Brave Enough to Share the Truth in Love*

LIONEL MESSI IS ONE of the greatest soccer players of all time and has won over forty major honors in his name at the team and international level.[1] The Chicago Bulls' Michael Jordan is known around the world as the greatest basketball player of all time. Los Angeles Dodgers' former pitcher, Orel Hershiser, holds the Major League record for most consecutive innings without giving up a single run—fifty-nine.[2] What do all of these men have in common? They were all cut from their high school and/or college teams! At that moment in time, someone had to share with them the difficult news that something was off, and they had some area they needed to work on to improve. Through commitment and perseverance, these men achieved great things. The words that were hard to hear at the time were used to shape these athletes for greatness.

Everyone wants to be liked, admired, and encouraged. It is much easier to share positive and encouraging things with brothers and sisters in Christ. However, when someone is struggling, it takes a true shepherd leader to share the truth with him. When referencing Eph 4:15, I find that people often focus on the active/action part of the verse and *not* the promise of the verse. "Rather, speaking the truth in love, we are to grow up in every way into him who is the head, into Christ." Yes, it is true we are to speak the truth of God's word into someone's life *in love*. However, fellow

1. Wright, "Messi Milestone Tracker," para. 7.
2. Baseball Almanac, "Orel Hershiser."

53

elder, why are we to do that? It is to have both parties grow more in the image of Christ! When we lean into this idea of speaking the truth in love, it is both the means of growing spiritually *and* the results of growing spiritually!

I would encourage you to use the following model on difficult shepherding matters where you need to be brave enough to speak the truth in love: PLEA.

Pray—Jas 1:5; Phil 4:6

Prayer should be the basis of all shepherding discussions. Men, we need to be guided by the power of the Holy Spirit in all things.

Listen Well—Jas 1:19; Prov 2:2

We need to not merely listen without speaking, we need to be *active* listeners. Our sheep need to know we are actively listening. My senior pastor is an excellent example in this area. He is not distracted by a phone or anything else. He looks at the people in his congregation with loving care, asks very few questions until they are completely done, and leans into the conversation . . . literally and physically.

Engage with the Truth—Eph 4:15; Isa 55:11

The truth of God will not return void, and when shared with your sheep, will return its purpose in their lives. Engaging a congregant with the truth, unfortunately, is the area where we sometimes need to engage more actively as elders. Why is that? Sometimes this is hard! However, be brave enough to have some Scriptures, whether memorized or studied, on the subject they are struggling with to share with them. God's word will do a work in their lives not only in that moment, but in the days and weeks ahead.

Actively Follow Up—John 10:14

This is key. John 10 mentions that a shepherd *knows* their sheep. How do you get to know your sheep? Spending time with them! Lovingly follow up with your sheep on the shepherding matter discussed with them. Shoot them a text after you have prayed for them with some Scripture you prayed for them. Don't leave that shepherding opportunity at the one "truth-speaking" moment. Follow through on it with love.

Speaking the truth in love is one of the hardest, and yet most loving, things we can do to help the sheep in our flock. Be willing to step in the deep end of shepherding and have these tough conversations. These conversations will be a blessing to both the sheep and the shepherd.

Discussion Questions/Application

1. Consider Eph 4:15 and "speaking the truth in love." In your experience, do Christian leaders lean more heavily on speaking truth or loving the person? Why?

2. What are the underlying reasons why an elder might lean towards loving a person instead of speaking truth, or vice versa?

3. In considering addressing difficult shepherding situations, which aspect of the PLEA model stood out to you the most?

4. Which aspect of the PLEA model do you think is the most countercultural today and why?

Part III—Shepherding the Shepherds

16. *Ask Hard Questions to Other Shepherds*

WHEN I WAS FIRST asked about serving as elder chairman, one of my concerns that I was processing was giving up some of my other discipleship responsibilities. The Lord quickly relieved me of that concern through the wisdom of the Holy Spirit. I realized that the elders on our board *were* my new disciples. They were men I was entrusted with shepherding, holding accountable, and asking the hard questions regarding their walks with the Lord. I was one of the younger elders, however I quickly realized they all desired that investment in their lives.

The other thing that the Lord impressed upon me as I served as chairman was the importance of shepherding this group. The enemy is strategic, and, while he wants to distract everyone from their relationship with the Lord, how much more likely is he to attack someone in leadership? As elders, we need to be ready for the attacks of the enemy. As a shepherd of shepherds, we need to invest time to ensure our elders are ready for that spiritual attack.

A few ways you can intentionally shepherd your fellow shepherds are:

Intentionally Pray for Them and Ask the Deeper Questions

Make a list of your elders, and pray for them and their families, specifically, on a regular basis. Make sure you also ask intentional questions to understand how God is teaching and challenging them. Some example questions might be, "What has God been teaching you through his word in the last week?," or, "How have you been able to serve your wife and children in the past couple weeks?," or, "Is there anything I can come alongside you and encourage you in at this time?" If you are going to invest time in your fellow elder, make sure the time is well spent and intentional.

Have a Specific Check-In Every Four to Six Weeks

Check in with each elder on your board, individually, every four to six weeks. Sometimes those check-ins can be with a face-to-face meeting. Some of those check-ins can simply be via phone or text message to find out specific ways they can be prayed for in the coming days and weeks. It is very important to segregate out specific time to reach out to each of them individually. This is another great time to intentionally ask the aforementioned questions of your elder team.

Encourage Your Fellow Elders

Hebrews 3:13 says "but exhort one another every day, as long as it is called 'today,' that none of you may be hardened by the deceitfulness of sin." As you get to know your fellow elders, you will learn what is going on in their lives and what they are struggling with daily. Take the opportunity to encourage (Heb 10:24–25) what the Lord is doing in each of their lives as he blesses them and gains victory over struggles or sin in their lives. Do not view them as someone who is just serving with you—view them as a brother in Christ who you do not want to be hardened by sin's deceitfulness!

Encourage Fellow Elders to Self-Reflect on Their Questions/Concerns

Oftentimes, when fellow elders feel passionate about any given issue, they must be able to express to the rest of the elders why they feel that way. Fellow elder, as you pray through an issue, ask yourself some of the following questions: "Is it a biblical conviction?" If so, we must all be in agreement. "Is the particular matter a personal conviction, based on biblical principles?" If so, it must be respected, but we need not always agree on that particular issue. We can agree to disagree. "Is it a personal preference?" If so, don't hold it too tightly; let it go.

Discussion Questions/Application

1. Consider the intentional questions listed above to ask fellow elders. Take some time to write out additional questions that would be helpful and fruitful in encouraging elders to pursue personal holiness and faithful serving.

2. Which of the listed ways to intentionally shepherd elders would you consider most important, and why?

3. Why is it important to encourage fellow elders evaluating an issue they're passionate about to consider whether it is a biblical conviction, personal conviction, or personal preference? Come up with a list of example topics or issues that could fall in each of those three categories.

4. Are there personal convictions or preferences that sometimes get confused with biblical convictions? Examples? Why, do you think, that can happen?

17. *Humbly Serve the Fellow Elder that Stretches You*

EARLY ON IN MY tenure serving as elder chairman at our local congregation, a highly respected brother in Christ who had previously served in a similar role said to me, "Be prepared; there will always be one that stretches you." I came to learn there was a tremendous amount of wisdom in that statement.

From an earthly perspective, the hope is for every individual on a team to get along, have unity, and experience very little conflict. However, the biblical perspective on how we grow in service to him is vastly different. Joseph had many trials in his life starting from a young age, not the least of which was being sold into slavery in Egypt. At the end of his life, after his father Jacob died, his brothers thought he would be repaying them for the past. Yet, Joseph said, "As for you, you meant evil against me, but God meant it for good, to bring it about that many people should be kept alive, as they are today" (Gen 50:20). Joseph grew through the challenges and trials that his brothers brought to him.

The same goes for us that shepherd other shepherds—there will always be one that helps us to grow in patience, leadership, and understanding. Though this can manifest itself in many ways, the following might be a few examples you could experience:

- As a group you're working through a position paper on a particularly complicated theological topic. All but one of your elders have consensus on the topic; however, one elder is adamant that his position is correct and will not yield to the consensus of the group.

- A particular elder has a passion project he would love to see the church focus on and continually brings it up to the group, despite the fact that the rest of the group is not behind that vision.

- A couple of elders require a significant amount of personal encouragement and shepherding outside of the scope of the meetings as they are uncomfortable sharing their positions in the meeting.

A shepherd of shepherds should handle these situations with the following steps:

1. *Pray.*

   Praying for discernment in handling any situation is wise. May we always be led by the power of the Holy Spirit.

2. *Discern if this is a biblical conviction, a personal conviction, or a preference.*

   Is the reason that the fellow shepherd is stretching you a clear biblical conviction or, simply, a personal preference? I had multiple conversations with a fellow elder about how passionate the church collectively was about a parachurch ministry he served with occasionally. He perceived an apathy from the church about the ministry area and was discouraged. We discussed discerning as elders what the best thing is for the church collectively as opposed to what our personal passions are, and that seemed to help. We also discussed bifurcating between our personal passions and passions for what's best for our congregation. Many of the items that make a fellow elder stretch his leadership are because of personal preferences or personal convictions. I would heavily discourage letting a personal preference hold up consensus of your elders. Allow me to be clear, if the elder has a clear biblical conviction he is concerned about that can be distinctly supported by Scripture, praise the Lord. God may have used this brother to help you in an area that is a blind spot theologically. However, typically that's not the case.

3. *Shepherd the elder, as appropriate, based on the circumstance.*

   Search the Scriptures with your fellow shepherd. However, if it is clear that this may be a personal preference or conviction, take time to shepherd that brother and work toward consensus by examining the Scriptures and the heart behind the issue. This shepherding work can take time and require patience. Everything in our secular culture wants us to rush to a conclusion. However, God calls us to be patient and grace giving and not to foolishly rush to move forward. "One who is wise is cautious and turns away from evil, but a fool is reckless and careless" (Prov 14:16).

4. *Be brave enough to speak the truth in love.*

   After you discern the Lord has given an appropriate amount of time to shepherd the brother through his personal preference or conviction, be confident in the Lord to lead. Speak the truth in love about moving forward for the betterment of the wider group and the church. Emphasize the importance of maintaining the unity of the Spirit in the bond of peace (Eph 4:3; 2 Cor 13:11; 1 Cor 1:10).

In shepherding shepherds, there will typically be one or two that will stretch care for your fellow elders. However, exercising patience and eager faithfulness (1 Pet 5:2) in shepherding can encourage a stronger bond of unity for your elder team. This bond can only enhance our "care for the church of God" (Acts 20:28) which, as elders, is our ultimate calling within the church.

Discussion Questions/Application

1. Consider the guidelines provided on how to shepherd one of your elders that is currently stretching you. Discuss how those guidelines are different than how the world communicates to handle challenging individuals.

2. What is a critical aspect of shepherding an elder through one of these difficult situations that may even involve a disagreement? Consider the following Scriptures in formulating your answer: Phil 2:3; Eph 4:3; 1 Cor 1:10.

3. Consider the importance of shepherding an elder based on the circumstance. Why would it be important for most of that shepherding to be completed outside of a typical elder meeting? Discuss why that is important to the elders as a whole, and also important to the individual that is stretching the chairman.

18. *Value People's Time and Service by Stewarding Time Well*

THE CONCEPT OF TIME is covered in many forms in the Scriptures. We are reminded that we have a finite number of days and we are to number them (Ps 90:12). We are to make the best use of the time God provides us (Col 4:5; Eph 5:16). Furthermore, if we are servants and followers of Jesus Christ, we are stewards of God's grace in all aspects of our lives (1 Pet 4:10). Why is it then, when becoming a shepherd to shepherds, we tend to throw the stewardship of time out the door? Who can relate to, or has experienced, one of the following examples?

- An elder meeting that started at 6:30 p.m. and scheduled to conclude by 8:30 p.m. continues until 11 p.m. and the elder chairman says, "Just one final item . . ."

- An elder meeting agenda that started with only two key shepherding items to cover and, yet, eventually nine topics are covered, including parking lot striping, types of lights in a Sunday school room, what we should do for pastor's tenth anniversary, etc.

- In the midst of a long meeting, an elder reflects while a fellow elder speaks: "Will we be here until 10 p.m. still listening to him brief us on the latest sermon he heard from his favorite preacher?"

Time is important, and the more time we drain of our fellow shepherds, the more discouraged and less effective we will be for service to the kingdom. Here are a few suggestions on how to value your fellow shepherds' time in their service to the local church.

1. *If the senior pastor is part of the elder board, the chairman and senior pastor communicate on agenda ahead of meeting.*

   Always make sure that you and the senior pastor are on the same page with the agenda. Prayerfully consider the agenda. If there are suggested agenda items from other elders, prayerfully consider inclusion in that meeting and make sure both parties are aware of that topic.

2. *Pray for consensus and wise decision-making.*

   Be committed to start each meeting in prayer for unity for the group and wisdom (Jas 1:5). Also, be open to the leading of the Holy Spirit throughout the meeting. There are some times that we need to just stop and pray to seek the Lord's wisdom.

3. *Stick to the agenda—no rabbit trails.*

   Two most desired ingredients for effective meetings are (a) setting clear objectives and (b) having a clear agenda. Be a strong shepherd to your team when other topics are brought up in the meeting after a moment of discussion by graciously refocusing the team back to the agenda.

4. *Work in subcommittees.*

   Don't work through items during the meeting with everyone. Management by group is not effective. Assign a subcommittee to work outside the scope of the main elder meeting, then have them present their updated findings for discussion and wisdom at the meeting.

5. *Strive for meetings that last less than ninety minutes.*

   Include prayer and devotion for the first fifteen to twenty minutes. The meeting itself should be no more than sixty to ninety minutes. A study of over one thousand individuals showed that the average person over the age of fifty can maintain their attention for fifty-eight minutes, while an individual thirty-five years or younger can maintain their attention for forty-five minutes.[1] If the meeting is going longer than ninety minutes, there is likely something that needs to be worked on in a subcommittee or a topic that needs a separate meeting. Lead your fellow elders in assessing that decision and making those decisions.

6. *Start on time.*

Often, as a leader, we want to make sure everyone is included. However, let us not forget we need to steward the time of those that have arrived on time, as well. Always start the meeting on time, or, at the latest, one to two minutes after the agreed-upon start time.

7. *Be a strong, but gracious, leader.*

Lead the elders in modeling prayer and patience, but also lead the team in encouraging consensus toward a decision. Graciously stick to the items above, and your fellow elders will respect that in the long term.

Discussion Questions/Application

1. Why does stewardship of your fellow elders' time matter?

2. The concept of elders working in subcommittees outside of regular meetings was discussed. Why is this important?

3. In your experience, which of the seven listed items on stewarding time is often the most ignored? Why?

4. If the senior pastor is part of the elder board, why is it important for he and the elder chairman to be in agreement on the agenda and topics prior to the meeting?

1. Davoult, "Professional Study," para. 7.

19. *Avoid People-Pleasing by Practicing Servant Leadership*

WE ARE THANKFUL FOR God's beautiful design in making man and uniquely creating each of us (Ps 139:14). That unique creation also comes with complications in relationship and serving as we all have different passion areas.

A group of elders may have the following areas of ecclesiastical passion:

- Supporting missions
- Hospitality
- Landscaping at the front of the church
- Engaging men and women in discipleship
- Political/cultural issues
- Overseas missions
- Children's ministry
- Coffee ministry

As a shepherd to shepherds and chairman, what a challenge to make all of these individuals happy! As a chairman, how do you ensure that you are a leader and not a people pleaser? Remind yourself of three key principles.

You Serve an Audience of "One"

While you are accountable to the Lord and the congregation, God appointed and called you to the role of chairman for a reason. Always remember that you are serving one Lord, one elder board, and one congregation. In a church of three hundred individuals, you cannot please three hundred people. However, you can do what is best for the church collectively. As the chairman of the elder board, you cannot make every individual elder pleased, but you can collectively work toward consensus. For your church, you can't make every congregant pleased; however, you can discern from the Lord through the counsel of many (Prov 15:22) the best decision for all. God's word is not the most popular direction to take from the world's perspective. Pray, seek counsel, and trust that the Holy Spirit will guide you. Please the Lord with your decisions and the congregation/flock will be just fine!

Think of the Others You Are Serving

A people-pleasing chairman will focus on making sure each individual's topic or concern is addressed. Addressing that individual's tangential matter may make that individual happy but doesn't take into account the other men around the table. In graciousness, the other elders may not say anything, but the remaining men are looking for you to lead and move past that topic. Oftentimes, through testimony of elders that have shared with me, they are sitting there thinking, "This is not on our agenda . . . let's move on, I would like to go home!" It takes a brave leader to gently and kindly move past a topic and carry the group forward. Be gracious to everyone, but not everyone's particular tangent can be addressed. Lead in a servant way that is best for the elder group as a whole.

Hands to the Plow

"Jesus said to him, 'No one who puts his hand to the plow and looks back is fit for the kingdom of God'" (Luke 9:62). As shepherd of shepherds, elder chairmen need to be keenly aware of the balance between graciousness and keeping our hands to the plow. Some of the "people-pleasing" topics that arise for elders are related to the past. Revisiting a prior shepherding item, discussing why a previous decision was made, or discussing a tangent related to something that's on their minds are all distractions. A chairman needs to be careful to not waver to the side (tangents) or look back too often but keep the group's hands to the plow to serve the Lord well.

Brothers, it may feel good to try to please everybody on your board, but as mentioned, remember we are serving an audience of one, Jesus Christ! Honor God with your decisions and hear out your fellow elders as best as you can, but be brave to move forward to advance the work of God's church!

Discussion Questions/Application

1. Why is pleasing people a tendency for Christian leaders, and, specifically, shepherds of shepherds?

2. How can an elder chairman strike the balance between making people feel valued and moving forward on an issue of importance for the group?

3. Consider the concept of serving an "audience of one" versus individuals in the congregation. How does that reframe your thinking of leading on a particular issue?

20. *Stand Behind Your Pastor and Hold Him Accountable*

SERVING AS A SENIOR pastor can be an incredibly fulfilling but often lonely vocational calling. If we were to ask our senior pastors, don't be surprised if they suffer with a lot of doubts and concerns. The enemy will often try to exploit that in the hearts of our pastors. As shepherds to shepherds, it is extremely important to balance between standing behind our pastors while also holding them accountable. They are both extremely important.

Stand Behind Your Pastor

Our pastors have a lot of shepherding challenges. Depending on their personalities, they will ingest, and empathize with, the challenges and struggles of their flocks at varying degrees. Our pastors often, unfortunately, are also the subject of criticism and critique. A pastor needs to protect the unity of the church while at the same time caring and shepherding. Sure, if married, they will get some of that care from their wives. However, the next line of defense—is you! Your pastor needs to know that you are a safe place they can come to for encouragement and that you will stand behind them. Be careful not to treat your pastor as an employee. He is a fellow elder, so encourage him and support him!

1. *Schedule at least a semi-monthly meeting with your senior pastor.*

This meeting should be focused on caring for him and seeing if there are things presently weighing on him. This meeting should *not* be focused on church life. If they are facing criticism or attack, assess if that criticism or attack is biblical, reasonable, and warranted.

2. *Assess if you need to meet with the individual criticizing or attacking your senior pastor.*

   Far too often I have seen firsthand that these situations are left unaddressed between the senior pastor and the member or regular attender of the church. We need to be willing to shepherd and encourage our senior pastors, especially when they may be receiving false criticisms. If appropriate, have another elder go with you as well. When left unaddressed, this is very debilitating and discouraging to senior pastors to see their elders not supporting them. Work with both the individual and the pastor to discern between biblical truths in the situation and personal preferences. Encourage both sides to assess what God is teaching them through this interaction.

Hold Them Accountable

While it is critical to support our pastors, it is also critical to hold them accountable. According to Brandon Billings in his thesis at Belmont University, one of the critical downfalls of larger churches is their lack of accountability structure.[1] In his research, he notes that an accountability structure that includes a plurality of elders and leaders with a "willpower to enforce accountability"[2] is key to ministry success. Consider some key ways healthy accountability can be maintained between the elders and the senior pastor:

1. Do not over-centralize decision-making. Ensure that the plurality of elders is making the vast decisions by consensus. This will be covered further in another section.

---

1. Billings, "Megachurches Can Have Mega Problems," 48.
2. Billings, "Megachurches Can Have Mega Problems," 64.

2. Be willing to tell your senior pastor the truth, even when it hurts him to hear it.

3. Work with your senior pastor to develop a list of hard questions he wants you to ask each time you meet.

4. Be an encourager to your senior pastor and have a listening ear in order to spur him on in his vocational ministry.

Striking the balance between standing behind your senior pastor and holding him accountable is a tension that will be a blessing to not only the church, but also to your senior pastor as he strives to be an example to his flock (1 Pet 5:3).

Discussion Questions/Application

1. Why is investment of time and encouragement in your senior pastor critical for their success in the role?

2. Pastors are criticized, often unjustly. As an elder, that criticism needs to be assessed in light of the Scriptures. Discuss a biblical model for addressing criticism of a pastor from those in the congregation. Consider 1 Tim 5:17–20 and Matt 18:15–20 in formulating your answer.

3. There are a grievous number of pastoral failings that make it into the news cycle. Sadly, they're all too familiar to us. These failings emphasize the importance of not only encouraging our pastors, but also holding them accountable. In considering that accountability, what do you think are the most critical responsibilities of an elder chairman and an elder board in pastoral accountability?

21. *Be Leery of Over-Centralizing Decision-Making*

DECISION-MAKING IS DIFFICULT AS a group. We are all unique individuals that have been woven together by God (Ps 139:13). In recent years, there has been a pattern within the church to move to a more centralized decision-making process.

An example from my own backyard is the case of Harvest Bible Chapel. After many years of growth, its pastor, James Mac-Donald, went from a plurality of elders making decisions to over thirty elders to an executive committee. The committee was comprised of himself and four to five other elders.[1] That change led to decreased accountability, a series of questionable financial decisions, and the eventual release of MacDonald as the senior pastor. Another church I am familiar with has an elder board of approximately six men covering their multiple campuses and thousands of regular attenders. This group also includes the two lead pastors. These are both examples of centralization of leadership.

Churches typically start to centralize decision-making after the following progression:

1. Ministry is off to a good start, and things are progressing well.

2. Ministries start to venture into different areas of ministry, not only practically but also geographically.

---

1. Roys, "Hard Times at Harvest," para. 22.

3. With that expansion is the need to have elders over the entirety of the ministry who have purview of everything.

4. Ministry continues to grow, so centralization becomes even more focused to a smaller group to allow for even more efficient decision-making.

Purely from a secular perspective, I can completely understand how ministries realign their decision-making and shepherding around these principles. However, as shepherds of the church, we need to base our decision-making and leadership model on the word of God, not secular wisdom. In reviewing relevant Scripture, the following principles are important in decision-making as it relates to church leadership:

1. *A plurality of elders*

   The Bible speaks consistently of the elders of the church in a plural sense, but they are always connected to a particular congregation. While the Scriptures do not specifically outline the exact number of elders it is consistent about a plural number of elders in shepherding the church (Acts 11:30; 14:23; 20:17; 21:18; Titus 1:5; Jas 5:14).

2. *There are not "classifications" of elders.*

   The Bible does not speak to different classes of elders when it comes to shepherding the church. The responsibility belongs, collectively, to the elders. The modern movement of executive teams or subsets of elders does not evidently appear in Scripture.

3. *The importance and value of a wide range of wisdom*

   The Bible speaks extensively about the importance of wisdom through a multitude of counselors. This is especially evident throughout the Proverbs (Prov 11:14; 13:10; 15:22; 20:18; 24:6). If there is a topic that the elders are discussing and it's not your area of expertise, call someone with that area of expertise! That person could be an elder chairman who served at another church. This person could be someone with expertise in shepherding the staff through adding ministries. These are just a couple examples. Reaching out to those with different skills and wisdom can lead to a much wiser decision (Prov 15:22).

4. *Help protect the church and the senior pastor against pride.*

The more centralized that the decision-making becomes, the leaders risk becoming less focused on what God is doing and more focused on what the leader is doing. It is healthy for a senior pastor to have decentralized decision-making because it guards against a narcissistic personality developing in an individual.

Decision-making can be more difficult as a group and, at times, even more time-consuming. However, God wants us to do hard things and do them prayerfully with wisdom. "One who is wise is cautious and turns away from evil, but a fool is reckless and careless" (Prov 14:16). May we, as shepherds of the church, cautiously pursue biblical wisdom in our decision-making.

Discussion Questions/Application

1. What are the typical arguments for centralization of decision-making at a church? In your experience, are those typically coming from Scripture or the world?

2. As discussed, the Bible talks about a plurality of elders and not centralized decision-making. What are the risks of centralized decision-making to the church and also to the individual serving as pastor or senior pastor?

22. *Plan for the Future*

WHEN I WAS GROWING up my father used to say to me all the time, "Poor planning leads to poor execution." It has stuck with me to this day. When it comes to shepherding the church, planning for the future is an oft-neglected aspect of elder leadership. With individuals serving as lay leaders, tyranny of the urgent is typically the order of the day. As the shepherd of shepherds, we need to keep the future in the forefront of our fellow shepherds' minds. Planning for the future for the senior pastor role is important, and often neglected.

The Barna Group did a research study in 2019 on pastoral transitions, and the data was alarming. Only 17 percent of pastoral transitions were planned. A whopping 62 percent were pastor-initiated and 21 percent were a variety of other reasons, including a pastor being removed from their role.[1] David Kinnaman, president of Barna Group, stated, "Successful leadership transitions require careful planning. . . . Planned departures go more smoothly, while forced or unplanned transitions are worse on multiple outcomes."[2] The planned transition usually completed within a year (73 percent) whereas unplanned only saw 53 percent accomplished in under a year.[3] This planned transition, from the congregation's perspective, produces significantly faster acquiescence of the new pastor into the congregation and feeling that he is their pastor. This

1. Barna, "Planned Pastoral Transitions," para. 3.
2. Barna, "Planned Pastoral Transitions," para. 6.
3. Barna, "Planned Pastoral Transitions," para. 6.

positive outcome through a planned transition, within a year, is far more expedient than what many friends in pastoral ministry say take typically three to five years to accomplish.

In leading your group of elders, there are a few wise things you can do to set up the future of your congregation to flourish during a pastoral transition.

Always Have a Long-Term Strategic Plan and Review It Annually

One of the best ways to plan for the future is always to be planning for the future. Yes, that sounds funny; however, many churches conflate the terms "strategic plan" and "annual goals." The strategic plan should cover a period of at least three to five years, and the goals are derived according to that plan. If a church has a solid strategic plan, it already knows the direction it senses the Lord leading, which can help with pastoral transitions.

As Your Senior Pastor Gets Within Ten Years of Retirement, Start the Hard Discussion

As the lead shepherd (chairman) on your elder board, be bold enough to initiate this conversation with your senior pastor as he starts getting closer to retirement. Shepherd your elders through planning for what that might look like long-term. Do not be shy in having the conversation because the aforementioned data shows that congregations thrive through planned transitions far greater than unplanned transitions.

In Looking to the Future, First Look Within the Walls of the Church Prior to Looking Outside

The depth and breadth of relationships is so critical in shepherding. When thinking of the future, it is wise to look within your own congregation. Pastor friends of mine have told me numbers of anywhere between three to five years when they truly feel that the church is their church, and the congregation has embraced him. You combine that with an average search time for a senior pastor of twelve to eighteen months,[4] and you are looking at over five years until the pastor feels at home! I would encourage assessing with your senior pastor along the way who the next senior pastor could potentially be from the current staff. A humble pastor will be willing to have this conversation.

Discussion Questions/Application

1. Do churches typically focus on planning for the near-term or the long-term? Why do you think that is the tendency?

2. Why is strategic planning so important for a church, and how effective do you believe your local church is in conducting that planning?

3. Who should bear the most responsibility when it comes to strategic planning in the church? Senior pastor? Elder chairman? Elder board as a whole?

4. National Association of Congregational Churches, "Pastoral Search," para. 10.

23. *Stay in Your Lane and Don't Leapfrog*

PERHAPS YOU REMEMBER YOUR childhood games of leapfrog. One player stands behind and as someone crouches down in front, the individual proceeds to push off that person's back in front of them and leap in front by passing the stages in between. While it was fun as an eight-year-old child, it can potentially prove to be dangerous and undercutting to a healthy church environment when used with a senior pastor's staff.

The elder chairman can hold different responsibilities. At our congregation, he is entrusted with leading our congregational meetings, our elder meetings, and our deacon meetings, shepherding those groups and maintaining a close working relationship with the senior pastor as they're invested in all the same things.

So how does this all intertwine with the call to not leapfrog? Fellow elder chairman, please don't leapfrog over your senior pastor and start instructing their staff what they should do, whether explicitly or implicitly.

Practice Discernment on What You Share with the Pastoral Staff, Implicitly and Explicitly

As a shepherd to shepherds, practice discernment in conversations with staff about specific responsibilities. This can apply to both explicit instruction or implicit guidance. Avoid having a breakfast or coffee to discuss specific tactics that a staff member should implement. You may be attempting to be kind to the person but at the same time undercutting your senior pastor! Implicitly exercise caution as well. As an example, you are aware the children's pastor is currently discussing with the senior pastor the missional purpose around the children's church program. At a gathering, it would be unwise for you to casually share your perspective on one viewpoint or another as that could be implicitly giving some guidance to the staff member. Encourage your senior pastor to lean into those discussions along with any input he receives directly from you. That approach encourages his leadership.

Check Your Heart on Motive

This is a subtle way that we need to make sure we do not participate in discouraging church unity. We are all human and have our own preferences when it comes to church ministry. However, as you pray about your heart before a conversation with your senior pastor, pray that the Lord would give you his wisdom on what is best for the congregation. Check your heart with transparent prayer to ensure that you are not providing what would be best for you.

Have an Open Dialogue with the Senior Pastor, Both Ways

Inevitably, conversations with staff members do occur. If you are actively engaged in 1 Pet 5:2 shepherding, a topic can come up about the tactical nature of an area of responsibility in church ministry. When it occurs, encourage them and also graciously redirect them to the senior pastor. If you have those conversations, I believe it is also wise to be transparent and to share that information with your senior pastor at your next meeting together so he is aware of it.

While innocent conversations with a church staff member can be well intentioned, always be mindful that the enemy is prowling around, and we want to strive for unity in our churches and our staff members. Keeping a watchful eye over our own leapfrogging encourages our senior pastors.

Discussion Questions/Application

1. What are the potential pitfalls of yourself (as chairman) or one of your elders discussing tactics with a particular member of the church staff? Have you experienced this situation?

2. What are the key ways to have a healthy dialogue and provide feedback to the senior pastor about the staff while not undermining him as a leader?

24. *Don't Buy into the False Narrative—*
If You Are Always Winning,
You Are Never Losing

OUR WESTERN CULTURE DRILLS information into us by affirming
the desires of our hearts through advertising. We want to be liked
and loved and want to be part of something that is successful, so as
such, we are drawn to things that present themselves as successful.
For example, the following chart shows two *different* ways (A and
B) that a ministry can communicate the same information update
to their congregation. When reading columns A and B, assess
which of the following comparatives would have a greater draw
of your attention or excitement (these are real examples but with
names and locations changed):

Ministry Area	Example from Church "A"	Example from Church "B"
Foreign Missions	What was communicated to the church: As a church, we've planted a church that has grown to 1,200 people in a certain foreign country. (What *actually* happened: The church simply contributed $2,000 to a church planter who served there for a week.)	What was communicated to the church: As a church, we've been able to participate in a church plant that has grown to fifty people in a certain foreign country. (What *actually* happened:– We've sent five teams of at least twenty people over the last five years to serve that mission.)

Ministry Area	Example from Church "A"	Example from Church "B"
Evangelistic Efforts of Our Local Church	What was communicated to the church: As a congregation, we've seen one thousand people come to Christ in the past two years. (What *actually* happened: Nearly 950 of those conversions were in the mission field, internationally. Fifty were at the local church in America.)	What was communicated to the church: As a church, we've seen one hundred people come to Christ in the past two years. (What *actually* happened: Nearly all of those conversions were in our communities surrounding the local church.)

Which column, A or B, is more appealing to include in a church advertisement? I think we all know that far too often column A makes it into the church materials and announcements. Why is that? There is a pressure to communicate large numbers and success to portray the wider success of the church "brand" . . . even if that means softening the edges of the communication. As the example above, it is much more exciting to communicate one thousand souls won to Christ (and that *is* exciting!); however, when done in a context of encouraging people to come to a local congregation, it comes across a bit disingenuous.

We have to be mindful to be transparent in all things as we lead our fellow elders and shepherd our congregation. I have been very concerned in the trend in recent years to "market" our churches as a brand or marketing tool to continue to show congregants they are getting a return on investment (i.e., return on their tithe giving). Far too often this branding is done with what, I would argue, is truthful, yet slightly deceptive, information.

The Christian walk and our ministries are filled with ups and down, and God calls us to rejoice in both the joys and sufferings. We need to be truthful and transparent with our congregations and, more importantly, before a holy God. God alone deserves the glory for the work in and through our churches and ministries. If we rejoice in our sufferings (Rom 5:3), then we also get to give God the glory when we see what he is teaching us through those moments. It may not lead to more people attending or more donations in that moment, but it will reap a harvest in the right time (Gal 6:9).

Personally, this goes for us as we also lead our fellow elders. We need to model for them transparency of what is going well and not going well in our lives. This will give your elders the freedom to live a life of transparency and openness with you. Do not sugar-coat your life and try to provide a rosy-colored picture when it is not that rosy.

We are all works in progress (Phil 1:6) until we see Jesus face-to-face in glory. We are being transformed into the image of Christ (2 Cor 3:18). Let us live out that reality before our churches and fellow elders.

Discussion Questions/Application

1. Why do you think there is a temptation within churches to communicate that we are "always winning?" If you find yourself in that situation at your local congregation, how can that cycle be broken?

2. What is an elder board's role in encouraging transparency and truth in communication regarding how the church is doing?

25. *Share and Then Work to Consensus*

SHARING AND COMMUNICATING IS key to effective relationships. Whether in a business setting, church setting, or family relationships, effective communication and gracious listening is important to a healthy relationship. It's important that we don't think of a question in our minds as a dumb question; we need to feel comfortable sharing, in love, what the Holy Spirit is prompting us to say (Eph 4:15).

When working with a group of elders, it is important to emphasize open communication and working toward consensus. As an elder, your role is to encourage your fellow elders to share biblical thoughts that they have on a topic with one another. If you are serving as chairman, your role is also to work with this divergent group of men with varied gifts and extract their wisdom as you work toward consensus. Our elders vote on very few things, which I believe is wise. We discuss until we have a consensus on an issue. The reason is simple: in voting there are winners and losers. In a consensus model of governance, everyone owns the decision once consensus occurs. In spite of their personal opinion, when consensus is reached the elders support the decision when leaving the meeting room for the health of the church and to protect the unity of the board and the congregation. While it is true that sometimes this will take longer, we do not want to be foolish and rush something (Prov 14:16) to be efficient at the expense of unity.

However, if after considering perspectives there is an individual who is still struggling, he needs to agree to fold himself in with his fellow elders. Your role as shepherd to the shepherds sometimes requires additional work in this area, especially if someone is having a hard time yielding to the consensus. With the principle of consensus, everyone gets to present his perspective. Meet with that brother and talk through it with him separately, searching the Scriptures together. However, if it is just a preference and not a doctrinal issue, then encourage him to fold into the consensus of his fellow elders. To that end, consensus is not unanimity. It just means that all the elders consent to that decision to move forward and will support it.

Lastly, if the group is stuck and cannot reach consensus, shepherd the group by giving further room for the Holy Spirit to work in the group. God is always working, and pray that the Lord reveals where he is leading your group. Take a break for prayer as a group and table the discussion until the next meeting. When you pick up the topic at the next meeting, state where there was consensus and the open item that was still being prayerfully considered in order to focus on that area of discussion.

John MacArthur cogently describes the concept of consensus as follows: "If there is division among the elders in making decisions, all the elders should study, pray, and seek the will of God together until consensus is achieved. In this way, the unity and harmony that the Lord desires for the church will begin with those individuals he has appointed to shepherd his flock."[1] I could not agree more; unity and harmony are key descriptions of what we strive for in leading our elders and our churches.

Discussion Questions/Application

1. What is the risk of voting versus working towards consensus? Why does this distinction matter?

2. Does consensus of the elder board mean unanimity? Why or why not?

---

1. MacArthur, "Biblical Eldership," para. 9.

3. In making a decision as a group, does timeliness matter in making that decision when trying to reach consensus? Why or why not? Are there situations where timeliness would matter more than others?

4. If you have previously served as an elder, have you ever experienced an issue on which the board had troubles achieving consensus? How was that resolved?

5. How does prayer impact this concept of working towards consensus? How can prayer impact this process individually, and collectively, as a group?

Bibliography

Barna. "Planned Pastoral Transitions Lead to Better Outcomes." August 6, 2019. https://www.barna.com/research/pastoral-transitions/.

Baseball Almanac. "MBL Stats for Orel Hershiser." https://www.baseball-almanac.com/players/player.php?p=hershor01.

Billings, Brandon. "Megachurches Can Have Mega Problems—Insights from Toxic Leadership in Modern Megachurches." Belmont University, April 4, 2020. https://repository.belmont.edu/honors_theses/7/.

Davoult, Thibault. "Professional Study: Managers' Attention Drop 52' into a Meeting." Solid. Apr. 2, 2015. https://www.getsolid.io/blog/meeting-attention-span-data.html.

DeYoung, Kevin. "What Does It Mean for an Overseer to Be 'Above Reproach' and 'Well Thought of by Others'?" The Gospel Coalition, April 27, 2016. https://www.thegospelcoalition.org/blogs/kevin-deyoung/what-does-it-mean-for-an-overseer-to-be-above-reproach-and-thought-of-well-by-outsiders/.

Dictionary.com. "Character." https://www.dictionary.com/browse/character.

Indeed. "Board of Director Title (and Board Member Job Descriptions)." March 26, 2025. https://www.indeed.com/career-advice/finding-a-job/board-of-directors-titles.

Jennings, Mike. "Best Job Site of 2025." Tech Radar, March 17, 2025. https://www.techradar.com/best/us-job-sites.

Keller, W. Phillip. A Shepherd Looks at Psalm 23. Grand Rapids: Zondervan, 2008.

MacArthur, John. "Biblical Eldership." Grace to You. https://www.gty.org/library/articles/GCCDD01/biblical-Eldership.

McKay, Adam, dir. Anchorman: The Legend of Ron Burgundy. Universal City, CA: DreamWorks Pictures, 2004.

Merriam-Webster. "Pride." June 7, 2025. https://www.merriam-webster.com/dictionary/pride.

National Association of Congregational Churches. "Pastoral Search." https://www.naccc.org/resources/pastoral-search/.

Roys, Julie. "Hard Times at Harvest." World News Group, December 13, 2018. https://wng.org/articles/hard-times-at-harvest-1617297601

Squires, Josh. "Pride Is Your Greatest Problem." Desiring God, July 29, 2015. https://www.desiringgod.org/articles/pride-is-your-greatest-problem.

Wright, Chris. "Messi Milestone Tracker: 800 Goals for Argentina, Barca, PSG." ESPN, March 28, 2023. https://www.espn.com/soccer/blog-the-toe-poke/story/4874225/lionel-messi-milestone-tracker-psg-barcelona-argentina.